Mrs Romanov

Mrs Romanov

LORI CAYER

The Porcupine's Quill

Library and Archives Canada Cataloguing in Publication

Cayer, Lori, author

Mrs Romanov / Lori Cayer.

Poems.

ISBN 978-0-88984-417-9 (softcover)

1. Alexandra, Empress, consort of Nicholas II, Emperor of Russia, 1872–1918 — Poetry. I. Title.

PS8605.A94M77 2018 C811'.6 C2018-904464-0

1 2 3 • 20 19 18

Published by The Porcupine's Quill, 68 Main Street, PO Box 160, Erin, Ontario NOB 1TO. http://porcupinesquill.ca

Readied for the press by Stephanie Small.
Interior images are after engravings from *Picturesque Europe* published by Cassell, Petter & Galpin, London, 1879.

Represented in Canada by Canadian Manda.
Trade orders are available from University of Toronto Press.

We acknowledge the support of the Ontario Arts Council and the Canada Council for the Arts for our publishing program. The financial support of the Government of Canada is also gratefully acknowledged.

For Todd Besant, my first and last reader, editor, supporter.
Without him this book would not exist.

The past is a dream, all earthly things slip away

... guards bang our doors at two a.m., urgency proliferates
like moonlight in the air, rush downstairs to safety

stiff as bitten teeth, sleep-addled and confused
another leave-taking, rumbling trucks outside

lined up, our backs against the wallpaper, a face of bad news
steps forward, reads a proclamation

his hand is a gun going off ... he seems to have shot Nicky
did he just shoot Nicky dead?

the side of my head jerked by cracked lightning
plaster behind erupting with sprayed stars

I am gone where light explodes, the room
all thunder

my empty hands flit, birdlike, looking for a place to land
I hear my girls screaming

their bulletproof bodices sewn in with our jewels
now they are being stabbed with bayonets

a windy sound inside me, pictures of our recent days
fading, shutting like an eye

*

a man must chop wood to feel busy and alive
freed from the body's detained grasp

a boy must play even under gunpoint
must parry and lunge and save the day

young ladies must wait and wonder if true love will come
and open their gilded doors

a mother must gather them finally; the table is set
the cloth is heaped with charred bones and dirt …

How unbearably white
The blind's white deep.

Anna Akhmatova

Each room as we left it, befallen

my list of dead begins before memory
baby brother tumbles from a window

a blood-flower blooms in his head
and puts him down to sleep

mama
mama screaming into her pillow

little sister only four, my own sweet playmate
giggling girl, puffs out, a fevered candle

mama
mama turns stone-blank and silent

goes straight to bed burning hot, forbidden to go near
her wet wet breath

past my room, her blanket-body is carried
sleeping

my dolls taken and burned up, my toys, blankets
clothes, even my pillow replaced, all unfamiliar

I crash through, soon after
roar and run across the low roof of the greenhouse

*

my small legs glass-cut, ribbons of flesh, ribbons of bandage
after: pain is my reliable dog

papa, my moon and sun—I am his third hand, his aide-de-camp
then he too, all in a moment face-drooped and limp, unbreathing

like a terrible garden, each plucked roughly up
round red radishes, stringy from the dirt, and tossed

I am crouched, looking down into dry holes
my self upturned, acutely into light

When I think of Granny, she is not the Queen of England

she does what any mother would do
for children who must wake up alone in their bodies

she has grandchildren to raise from a distance called Germany
a distance of daily letters and hand-picked nannies

our hands grip across two weeks of hard water
that's how long it takes to see her in her fleshy glory

her attention a definitive ringing like church bells
she turns this motherless child as English

as tea and crumpets, as pious as crumpets without jam
she passes the iron corset of fortitude and cold rooms

she passes like a square of lace
the idea of loving a man

Love opened in my belly, like God's sore wings

his northern eyes hang on me like loosened silk
blue as the sky's imagination; he sees me entire

my eyes reply *There you are*
my shyness at the edges of raucous rooms

evaporates next to his timbre of cello, his body
a poised animal in its wool and brass

and we two
just old enough to feel something not childish

a bit older, he leans me hard
against a garden wall

*

I want nothing more, but when he asks I find
I am an edifice, a marble monument

my God holds me back like a curtain
a nun married to my brown country's faith

even the Kings and Queens I know cannot convince me
I refuse his hand I don't know how many times

*

then his father dies, and in a day Nicky
is a Tsar given by God to Russia, ready or not

a wife, ready or not, is given to a man in sore need
he will be my good endeavour, my rod of helping

hand to God, hand to my husband's dear cheek
love is not innocent: love must succeed

What has passed has passed, and will never return

to make a man of Nicky, his father and the uncles
selected the ballerina Mathilde

of course not a whore by trade
but with the whore's undressed education

such is the tainted thinking of old men
unprepared for a woman's scorned heart

her fool's heart, that is, thinking itself in love
with an Emperor-in-waiting

meanwhile he also loves me, all unknowing
years of letters from a girl in a glass ball

his letters back
from behind a gypsy's swirling veil

so garish his abject maleness exploding
like gunpowder, like a dashed-apart wineglass

*

the day I agree to marry him he ends with her
gives her a mansion for a keepsake

I learn of them, because she sends me letters
from *No-one*

filthy details of vodka and tobacco and pulled lace
I drop them in Nicky's lap, my eyes stinging like bees

our love, then, not a blessing of virgins
but a lie witnessed by God and all the Russian court

his shine-eyed confession
moves from my heart downward

Everything, so beautifully green-bright of flowers

our engagement is in the papers around the world
everywhere I go rude people stand

in the streets to stare and whisper
I have to come and go like a thief by a back gate

but I am ignited in my happiness, a sun-glare
that turns everything into a painting of my life

it is I who wins the prize
a husband with no need of a mistress

our souls welded fast
just us two, passing each blue hour till dawn

who can forgive what needs no forgiveness?
I have made a true home inside him, and he in me

such small insomnias of spirit must be released
back to the stream

Backward looking is for fools, and I was a girlish fool to let them

my wedding attire, for example, doubles my weight
I leave the room to weep of its bending me

pounds of ermine fur
miles of metal thread, silver and gold

necklace heavy as a tea tray, hooked over my ears by wires
someone paints this picture, my face of a small animal

*

the only thing the same about me is my hands
I am looking at them in church when I think God

must have forgiven me
but I only fainted because of the baby that didn't stay

this rupture of light, this flood of holy reckoning
which is my marriage

from here I begin again
not a vessel but an engine, a body pierced with love

My Russian faulty, the line of my mouth unable

the opulence here is shocking, makes England a fairy tale
and my home palace medieval when compared

don't I learn this country's ugly-tongue language?
its gilded religion smoky and sung by the drone of men?

I am already hardening, broken-edged, into pieces of duty
don't I daily attend strangers for whom I feel nothing?

try to falsely smile, my shyness a fish in the throat
knees buckling like a marionette?

Nicky's mother would create me in her stalwart image
her easy smile, her easy grace

she sends me bright dresses in her favourite colours
their sheer value drooping in my dressing room

how am I to ignore
the spleen of what they all say?

funeral bride, icy Queen, dowdy lower royalty
a hated German in their precious court

but I am German only by father
and the plain church I left behind

by mother and grandmother, their invisible legacy
I think in English first

He calls me precise, a needle pointing

from my first days I can see the truth
the father had broken the fine horse in the boy

drunk and cruel, each day off to the throne like a bear
leaving the wretched boy with its mother

her swaddling, wheedling ways
he taught the boy nothing of being a ruler

his mother is no better
a cliché of sweetness to my face

but the matter of the jewels sets us forever crossed
Nicky says, in our marriage bed, if only his brother

Misha had been born before him
Nicky could have stayed a plain soldier of the ranks

he is a bound spring, a roebuck on the fly
my man of thick books and head of five languages

*

now he visits his mother without me
she keeps him aloft between her palms

she and I have little use for each other, both of us
want that soft core of him for our own teeth

both of us talking, talking into his ears, his mind
a bell as yet unrung

I have tried to look, in every light possible

they think us puppets, and yes, at first our strings
can be pulled

coronation day sets the tone for our reign
a day begun with brocade and ended in hell's ballroom

our first public disaster, courtesy of the family
those arguing bullying beasts

the overcrowding is his uncle Sergei's fault
my sister Ella's vitriolic husband, hated by all

thousands of peasants with hope for a kinder regime
trampled and dead for the promise of free food and drink

we cancel the day to mourn with our people
and are forced by the ministers to dance at the ball

the people take home their dire beliefs
and stir them in a poor pot

this is the way we begin
dancing on orders, tongue-bitten

our painted eyes looking out the windows
at carts piled high with rough bodies

Show your own mind, and don't let others forget who you are

is it wrong that I feel a secret shame for my husband?
I can't bear to watch him, a fish on the sand

his father's men who use him for their own affairs
he inhales his rage with constant cigarettes

bends a hundred times a day
to the will of the one with whom he last spoke

twelve hours a day they bury him in mounds of papers
he diligently reads and signs every document

from banal approvals of Easter egg gifts for staff
to exiles and death sentences

is it love or my own nature that spurs me on?
husband of capitulation, husband of avoidant ways

I apply myself to him as a poultice of pressure
describe a fist, a voice, push him out the door

inside and out I see all are displeased with him
he aligns his pencils

stubborn like an abandoned old railcar
he is pushed squealing or he is frozen in place

I tell God I fear I have married not an Emperor
but a man in his ordinary cloak of skin

She advises me, Queen to Queen, to earn my people's respect

Alix Victoria Helen Louise Beatrice of Hesse-Darmstadt, my name
as long as my whole hand—am I

five women in one? Victoria is inside me
somewhere between spine and wherewithal

she can read the world's newspapers for herself
to see I am disliked without even a crime

Queen Granny and her advice, her lovely scrawl
which ink is also my heartbeat

dear Granny, you do not know Russia
here we rule by God's grace and expectation

the people live like lambs, loving their Little Father
I stand by your own example

the child imprisoned
the Queen who would exile her own mother

if Nicky and I were to rule differently
the world would have to begin again

My favourite colour mauve, a favourite flower lilac

the ordinary human things:
restraint is mother, order is mother

the girls get one gift at holy days and birthdays
new clothes when they are needed

each their own Brownie box camera
hand-sized personal apparatuses

from click to instant memories
photographs in our hands in a few short days

not Nicky with a camera though, he even refuses
telephones when everyone else easily uses them

spartan meals for every day
I wasn't raised English for nothing

I am mother to the simple people of the realm
peasants of pure autocratic temperament

anyone who could see into this house
would see love

breathing itself like a tubercular lung
imprinting itself to life like a snapshot

A fourth girl, a near death and no acquiescence

every year is the worst year after our first happy few
the dirty tricks of life took me out of my thinking

first Granny died when I was four months gone
the very Queen of England, her life of lost men

my every day forever without her
the black dress of her

then Nicky goes under with typhoid
but by God and by grace he will not die

and leave me like this
I am his nurse, bodyguard

humming thrive of beehive
damn them all and their beards

I declare myself his regent in place of his brother
until this baby confirms itself heir or girl

his body is draining out, he is a burning river
his skull teeth chatter; he shall not be seen in this state

I sit with him all the hours, my great moon of baby
rumbling near, I lock the door to his men

it turned out it was Anastasia in there
rolling like a bicycle, all legs and wheeling arms

In the henhouse, murmurs of sleeping feathers

four girls in six years, our enchanting imperial failures
they make Two Pairs: Big and Small, Older and Younger

I dress them alike, one white-plumed bird
crisp as freshly snapped flowers

my lap-of-newspapers talk of *narodniks* and *soviets*
Mensheviks and *Bolsheviks*

form and form again like river ice in autumn
weasels and wolves

licking clean the dirty faces, the lambs of our land
their promising smiles of teeth

for each Nicky puts down, a horde emerges
like red ants in the pantry

I have my own concerns, manifold and crushing
my luggage full, my mind a spilled-over furnace

together our girls are a detachment
a rupture of demure

Such a bad year, submerged like a sack of kittens

what happens with the 'baby'
causes a further undoing of my mind's stays

so badly I need to bring an heir
behind God's back I seek council in new thought

a mystic with the gift of sight
God told him I am pregnant and so

and so, and so I am
God also said to lock the doctors out

in nine months I deliver an embarrassment
of blood: no baby, no pregnancy at all

my mind has made it up, the belly
like a trickster, growing itself round

I am an endless flash of blinding light
my private soul burst apart like kaleidoscope glass

my body's silence blisters the light
how could He?

Nicky tells the papers *miscarriage*:
of my body and soul, I might have added

Enter into thy closet, and when thou hast shut thy door, pray

Matthew 6:6

I need something more than church, more than
harmonic drone and orthodoxy

I need a life created from my rib for all history
an act stronger than our wet prayers in the night

we turn together, Nicky and I, on our fallen knees
to the spiritualist who says

to receive a boy, we must glorify an ancient priest
travel to his church in the far provinces

and I should bathe my sore womb
in his sacred pool

spark God's gracious finger
to unfold my body's obstinate ache

imagine a mother's fury when the Church should refuse
to make a saint on orders, so obvious a solution

I tell those gliding gilded cloaks
Nicky can do anything he pleases and it pleases him

to calm me down with Godly acts of hope
even Ella comes with me to the icy waters, and like

the sweet motherless sisters we ever were, like nuns
we give ourselves wholly and painfully to God

When I think no-one can hear, for the keening

a new lady-in-waiting, barely a woman herself
eager to please like a dog or a lonely child

Anna eats my every word as sacrament
she is made of baby fat and delights in the children

I put her in a little house outside my gate
ever just minutes from my own lonely call

there is no shop, after all, for obtaining a friend
please may I have one, part sister, part daughter

my constant companion, my echo in the marble halls
we are a pair of crutches

our bond is a factory of secrets, infallible
her instincts about God and His deputies on earth

whatever I do, society quacks and the papers surmise
depict us with our hands in each other's dresses

their limited notions of ecstasy
thin as bodies, debased

Blood skeins through, like wet yarn

and then our boy is delivered, a hard short
destruction of the fruit basket

minutes old, Alexei wakes the land with his first
gunshots, three hundred (and one) for an heir

I have finally appeased the curled-up lips
of all who constantly watch us in our terrarium

milk and woollen lace, he is a good size
I tell him he is the coin of the realm

in the rooms of this house we are
a closed-up circle, unwrapping our gift

whatever happens now
we are saved by history's inoculating hand

beyond these walls a dark wildness ensues
I mark him, with all my senses alert

look how he shakes his life in little fists
how his little name will carry us on

Because today, this baby boy did not leave the world

as always I wonder why happiness is so fleet
a swift upward swing, lifted as by wings

then blood, next thing you know
blood soaking through the swaddling clothes

from his sweet navel, where I was last attached
the hours are filled like never before

I spill milk into him and he bleeds till he is limp
and sleepy

when I think I can endure no more
we close this house away from scrutiny

a long silence like snow covers this truth
from the prying world

*

I did this to my boy
as Granny's veins did to her own son

as done to my baby brother I never knew
and as to my sister's lost boy

my seat on the family tree indelible
this ruinous sceptre passed down

we mothers of bleeders
stand trembling amidst blood's indifference

This bell has rung from the light, its ringing will be with us forever

Grigory Rasputin

Anna proves a useful maven, her house a refuge
when my skittering humours can't bear the forest

of eyes and gossiping teeth; we creep there Nicky and I
and stay till the moon makes its bright way home

she brings the best theosophical minds
talk of mystic means to Godliness, a few friends

of God, a few women who seem to like me
Anna, like a procurer, presents us Grigory Rasputin

staretz, holy man, miracle in a stinking coat
prayers from His invading eyes

bring messages straight from God to my torn soul
still the spill of our boy's bleeding body

my act of rebellion: to feel helped
the boy released in tides of sleep

one thing the gossipers say is true
I dream of Him

entering me
a deep and brightly upward salvation

Our Friend calls me to God, a burst bruise

He is my Bible come to life
Our Friend unfolding His prophecies

cannily knowing exactly what I need to hear
I cup my palms before Him

receive the salvation
He spills like a bag of seed

Alexei hears Him from within his thrall of pain
a threaded droning, a purpled and hypnotic call

so mother may stop dying too, a moment
the doctors suffer His advice and stand down

blood retreats from where it does not belong
Alexei's swollen, splitting parts return to normal

this man is a Little Jesus come back to earth
in the simple mystic peasant

He empties our questions
and fills them instead with wonder

Broken iterations, toward a purified body

the boy, ever in a steady state of death-pain
the mother howling silently in a gorge of sorrow

there is no cure for the screaming at night
he runs and bleeding erupts between bones

cranks his knee to his chest
so he can't walk for months, he throws a ball

and his arm retracts into a rusted axle
I am not afraid, Mother, let it come

from state dinner parties I endure with sweating
lip, I gather my skirts high for running

the long halls to his room, tear off the jewels
re-enter the wound in which he scrapes

no-one can say we are not swallowed whole
by all this dying, then living again

No concessions from an angry man, his uniform face

the ministers decide a colonial taking of Japan
will distract the masses from revolution

I have my opinions, but also Alexei in arms
so I leave Nicky to his men

our soldiers fall, bags of meat, in bad boots
the people fight each other for bread

the same sky as before
looks down on the ugly bed of a lost war

at home the vat of revolution continues to spew
its yeast, false promises sift down

on blunt heads
like sheaves of paper released to the wind

strikes in the streets, a mob marches to our door
Nicky orders them mown like red grass

now the papers call him *Nicholas the Bloody*
not even home at the time

*

Nicky blames this brief revolution on the Jews
as did all the fathers before him

he blames the rebels and crushes them with his pen
of execution, pen of incarceration, pen of Siberian exile

the ministers force him to create a parliamentary Duma
he disbands it in a fit of autocratic pique

my darling, finally
husband of standing up, husband of discovering a spine

We cannot help the faces we were given

everything that happens can be traced
back to our faces, look at the photographs

both of us trained since birth, unmoving
for the long blink of the camera's eye

Nicky's face inscrutable, whatever his raging
or desiccated thoughts may be

my face of thin lips, pinch of brows
and deadly honest eyes

I cannot pretend if I want
and I do not want

along the way some loved ones die
some strangers

we are a correlated study in marble
or moonlight; all this to say

we are only savage
in certain light

Heavy trials everywhere, but at home in our nest, bright sunshine

revolution stamped out, we retreat
to Alexander Palace in its deep green park

there is no threat like assassination
or a child like a constantly setting sun

there is no cruelty like that of society women
they, in their low-cut gowns, mock my stumpy Russian

they laugh at my grey and mauve, those drab
secondary-mourning colours of my provincial clothes

what are they but next thing to harlots with their drinking
and dancing and flagrant habits?

French is the language of court so I speak it
I am a drained sac, I cancel all state events permanently

close off the family's overweening questions
it's little wonder I am cast away broken to bed

surrounded by a blurring of ten little hands
fifty little fingers tappity tapping

*

now Nicky can return from his offices
a moment's walk

from his end of our long wing
to our rooms at the other

here is my love home from work, his exhausted face
the children leap around him like colts

we are hungry for him
we have our whole days to tell

The heart all wrong, beating like a bird in a bag

who should know how it is for me, in this ruinous body
off my feet in this room or that

Nicky despairs that I am so prone
to my room, to my insistently talking tongue

everything that undoes me takes the form of a list
shimmering headaches, sore eyes from crying

and also from the pinched strain of not crying
the heart, that old painter, blue-tinting the lips

face and jaw shoot electric pains, hard biting-down
on thoughts before I let them out into the air

shall I continue? not one baby fewer than ten pounds
industrial openings of the body's great hinge

wires of pain down the back and legs
the doctors use words like *neuralgia, angina, sciatica*

add the word *hysterical* at every turn
I heard Nicky say *Better one Rasputin than ten fits*

of hysterics every day
now I am in bed inflamed by his words

*

his loneliness in the evenings hurts like an old bruise
I have drowsy medicines to sweep it all away

common opium, morphine, Veronal
Adonis drops for the grouse-winged heart

fanciful names for the dull blanket thrown over pain
dear doctor, dear husband

this body does its own work
enter my red chamber, step in here, I'll show you hysteria

A postcard flower for each, the way they really are

for Olga a reliable rose, pink or white
petals of kid leather, aloof in her glass
she is moral and severe, she wishes exactly
nothing that I wish, our two heads
a rumble of stones

Tatiana a single wafting daisy, long and slight
wire-stemmed, coming up like sunshine itself
to surprise the cracks and edges
sits the hours with mother, aims to please
no, we do not choose favourites

Maria, both hands filled with one enormous
peony, a fullness of lip, a forthrightness of voice
child of miasma
born between the ladies and the brats
heady love, love flagrant and love certain

Anastasia a burst of lilac
explosive infiltration of rooms
silly thing feels unwanted, not born an heir
bosses about the place in her stamping shoes
diplomatic as weather

Where the sun wakes up, a bluish-white heavenly body

we had a messenger from the Outside World
his story bursting from his fevered beard:

one morning the sky was blown in two
by a river of fire, burning wind exploded

between houses and tore up the ground
like being shoved, it blew the hut down around me

then a second sun came into the blue
morning sky, impossibly bright

God threw a stone as large as a crushed city
artillery of His heavenly body

at Siberia's dark northern forest
bright necklace of the Stony Tunguska River

all the trees were falling, branches on fire
others stood blackened, made naked

by God's burning eye
I saw it was the end of the world

*

or the world starting over, God shooting
across the bow, a warning to the impious

so I ran from my ruined home to seek solace
and ended here telling you this true thing

the skinned trees laid down in a thousand-mile circle
burnt reindeer scattered like kindling

and in the centre   nothing
for He blew up his invisible body there

The Inside World, where we have ever lived

perhaps I have been too hard on the older ones
my blood of dark tea and nannies

across a room my face guides them to correction
deploys harsh whispers or days of silence

no surprise they prefer the company of their father
walk on their heels and shout

*

our Inside World takes all year to visit each palace in turn
we bring all the trunks of photograph albums

three dogs come with us everywhere and our cameras
that third eye always ready in the hand

*

I am told Alexei is a very rude boy, entirely disobedient
that is what staff and sisters are for

what fathers are for
I am tired, and the boy is tainted by thin blood

I will not be the one
to diminish his time on earth

*

Inside Evenings, we sit together sticking photographs
felty pages, all our memories corner-wise stars

our cameras little wonder boxes of moving windows
light goes in, our uncanny shadows come out

record us as a series of facts
the distant cousins of clarity and certainty

He who is our imperfect, specific secret

we take Anna everywhere, even on holiday
a sloven and a shrew, I call her not fondly *The Cow*

paid only enough that I know her friendship is real
even if my own fades daily

if Our Friend is next to God, and I am on the settee
then she is the telephone wire

she who must be congratulated at every turn
for the introduction of Our Friend

lately Nicky only tolerates her and barely, Our Friend
the whole of Russia wants Him removed from court

from our daughters' nightgowned rooms
she remains useful if only

to bring Our Friend through a side door
when Alexei's episodes strike

I would like to say she is something beautiful
from nature like a rhododendron in drooping

bloom or a bird having just flown from its body
but such lies elude me

When he bleeds, there is so little blood

like guilt in a culpable soul, the bleeding takes place
inside the case of skin, molten bruises hot to the touch

it fills and stretches where there is no space for fluid
his knee a reddish-purple melon about to split

pain takes him ghostly under to the deathplace
his blackened eyes soot out the light

all the ways he can die without spilling a drop
what can be done is nothing but bed or a rolling chair

his ankle a wineskin full to bursting
he is purple-black, red-yellow

a bruise-garden beneath his clothes
for weeks a leg thick and unbendable as a carpet roll

when it stops and he learns to walk again
he is a normal boy

a lifelike puppet with joints of loose gravel
he is a crucible of eggshells

what can be done
is nothing

He is hated, because we love him

rascal, rogue, reprobate, rapscallion
His eyes mad Bible pages

skin dirty as a returning soldier
they think I don't know about His ways

the blue ointment, the disrobing matrons
eager to supplicate his philosophy of sin

braggadocio that He has our ears
I see His cleanliness of faith, penetrated by God

He brings messages from the future
virtue and sin cleave when He enters my door

to paw and grub my lace, a putrid thought
the woman of teeming flesh under this bodice

is a bundle of cords, tangle of every kind of pain
what He and I want together streams

out from the head, a clear line opened
to God's ear, the word entering

Our Friend like electric light
sudden blessings filling up the room

I have shut my eyes
my draperies, and abide in Him

To press my soul to paper, a flower in a wordless book

the Lady visits
with her tears and arguing moods

her specific hurting in the belly
aching a low throb or a high-pitched bending chime

a wide encompassing bubble of sadness
in which wafts, desolate, the whole self

with five of us plus Anna turning the moon
the house is a box of pecking hens

always someone's dramatic return to bed
colourless as a photograph for five days

behind the eyes the whole story, red ribbons unfurling
beneath the linens

Death bleed, Spala

Alexei's pale body emits a sound that flays the long nerves
his pain a white rending, inside a red war

we are broken upon this cross with him
travel with him toward his twisting death

no-one should hear their child's last sacrament
my every thought browning like an ended flower

a public announcement, no illness stated
a hush the size of the world falls like fog

*

from far at the bottom of these ecru nights
a tea-soak of sleeplike, violent wakings

Alexei rises up, aware it is coming, asks
if there will be a little monument on his grave

Our Friend telephones from Siberia: the little one will not die
keep the doctors away, their new-fangled Aspirin

my lungs exhale stars, my heart beats down the doors
oh my child, my words erase themselves from time

Nicky's biggest problem at home, fat Anna at his footstool

the very world has changed since those old days
in her parlour

it is now a place of machinery over muscle
a place of motor cars and airplanes

between the velveteen of old and new
we are pinned moths, ash dusted

a ship the size of a palace went down, a cup
of beads in a fountain

now she is here every day and evening
agreeing with all my words, flapping her eyes

touching Nicky's feet under the dinner table
I prod him to make her stop but he leaves her to me

my bossy scrutineer, petulant little sister
if I do not give her audience she whines

for our embroidery hours, our hymns and luncheons
she harangues me until I hate the size of her

like a trunk dragged into every room
I would cast her out but for her cache of our privacies

Grigory says, Grigory says
she sings His praises like a baby bird

To be like them, bound in tenderness

I explain to no-one the time needed alone
by those who have lived motherless

my boudoir door-shut like nobody home
a small hot flame in its familiar lamp

the children despair and write me room to room
soften their demands by asking on each other's behalf

Maria wants to know when will Delacroix come for the hair?
he has not been for so long

Alexei says that other boys have bicycles and he has none
when can Olga let down her skirts and put up her hair?

they wish for friends besides their servants
but I had none and grew up proper

they will not be influenced by the hedonism of people
of our stature, of people these days

they must learn: together become a single self
a tract of willow moving in the wind

Birch leaves, their dry piles of telegrams

the sound behind the quiet is a new revolution, arms
and legs never quite in the grave

now there is one called Stalin with his paper *Pravda*
its false name of truth

one foot always in jail, the other a boot in the teeth
am I the only one who sees?

one regime or another, the dead will remain
underfoot like wet carpet

meanwhile two continents are cut apart like so much cake
moving sleeves of photographs make us walk along

like bobbing birds, music pours out of fluted machines
inventions come at such blinding speed

our children do not remember our old slow world
plain books and lamplight

history is happening even as the sentence of each day ends
is this when I should say the journey is also the purpose?

our iron train cleaves the forest
marks a deep groove, leaves behind no trace

War, and I knew nothing of it!

the mouth of thc world is stunned open, date etched
Franz Ferdinand and Sophie shot dead

all of Europe playing deadly chess
cousin Willy has dismissed his own better soul

foot stamping Emperor of Germany
he visits in uniform, heels sparking

mongering war and mongering Nicky
one-armed bully inventing a new world of war

Nicky stands flat as a barn door
gargantuan brother to Serbia

*

Nicky tells me at dinner, talks have failed
we are no longer family when guns are pointed

Germany has declared war on us
that is to say Willy has declared war on Nicky

a spitting petulance of historic proportions
I collapse without words to the settee

Nicky has gone sheer
a pencil drawing of himself

From the crucible of my sufferings, my nursing certificate in my hand

this is the beginning of me standing
suddenly up from my sickbed and walking out

alive with good intentions; I become a Sister of Mercy
building the hospital trains is my consolation

the Little Pair of girls read to the wounded soldiers
the Big Pair become nurses and open hospitals

tending the wounded forestalls the aching mind
living bodies arrive stiff of mud and blood

manhood destroyed by explosions, the first task
medicate the screaming, rinse bloody dirt

even out of eye sockets, cut away the stinking
ribbons that were lately the clothes of boys

sew what we are given to mend, shut their opened bodies
close their eyes to the picture reels in their heads

pray over their breathing, that they live
the night without sepsis, fever or rot

*

I am as Russian as Siberia, as beets and vodka
as the boys whose severed legs I carry away

the country of my birth an embarrassment
Willy an enemy of the world and of me

watchers stand about outside our gates
with their cameras and dirty journalism

we put on our nursing habits at home
and sneak to hospital by taxi

pass before their stupid noses as nuns
don't we all believe in everything we believe?

My diary knows, I give her too much leave to speak

Anna's mouth is a bad habit, a battery of geese
her swerving moods, shouts and slammed doors

shrill critiques of me and Nicky, our official decisions
lashed at home by her tongue

now there is war she has created herself our gatekeeper
my helpmate of daily thorns

runs our words like a postman to Our Friend
returns with his advice

one day, her demented nerve
to declare herself in love with Nicky

and he with her, she the better choice of wife
his pictures in their dozens on all her tables

writes him besotted reams which he politely answers
and burns at my insistence

after bringing her into this family, these are the thanks?
she careens like a bat in the house, peeling my nerves

the doctor sends me back to bed, *without* visitors
she waits me out, devoted as a disease

Unseen, the harp string at my core

I move simply among my man and my children
as birches sieve and scatter the sunlight

my affection filters them, keeps them pure
they should rejoice in my strong and proper action

my two selves
bound to earth, made of fractures and leather

mother, splinter, wife, nurse, damned splinter
damnable Empress, splinter and shard

in my eyes, a true duty-book of restraint, knife edged
reflecting photographic tones, long seconds

unsmiling so the picture will not be blurred
but what of the men who will dig my grave?

my death dress, my code of privacies and sewn scars
the forms of my loving, scrawling forward across time

will they understand my splendid purpose?
the earth will never be rid of my bones

Forgive me, but I don't like the choice for Minister of War

there is so much at stake
it crushes Nicky's chest and beads his forehead

soldiers fall in their millions, no-one counts
the wives and children

I will not apologize for asking to be made Regent
while Nicky leads the war from the front

he's only a telegram away and I've told him
Use me, I have trousers on unseen

the sweet face of him then
demeanour of a man waiting in God's vestibule

he has too much, and what he puts his hand on
turns to pudding

Our Friend becomes my right hand, my advisor
together we more closely resemble God himself

I finally have the power to stub out those ministers
like so many filthy cigars

they look at me now with eyes opened to hell
like they think I will die before them

*

who does not resign, I dismiss, until all
are of my choosing

are amenable to Our Friend's wisdom
let them say I warmed my hands while a country burned

let them say I did too much and all of it wrong
let them

The dark individual, unnamed, who will ruin the world

Nicky owns most of the world but he cannot stop
the papers spinning their lies

Our Friend a rapist of nuns and children and widows
He is impotent, He is not

He is the real ruler of Russia, He is a spy
mongering unwanted peace with Germany

I demand Nicky disallow Our Friend's name in print
so they call Him the *dark individual*

gossip breaks daily like a sour blister
vile cartoons of Him and me *in flagrante delicto*

*

in truth I can see He does not help His own cause
His mania does not rest, His drinking worsens

He receives death threats and the secret police
follow his every movement, His orgies

His sideways theory of ecstatic personal cleansings
the more He sins, the more He can be forgiven

*

I tell everyone they must see the good man in Him
who might have had another life if not for poverty

peace worker, voice for the poor, God rest
the idea, a different kind of revolutionary; instead

He makes his own electric cloud and twitches within it
paranoid, bellowing, incredulous

The soul of thy handmaiden, Lord

Russian Orthodox prayer for the dead

who has not come to demand Our Friend's removal?
insisting themselves on me for hours

among them Nicky's mother, my sister Ella
they must think themselves prophets, too

declaring me lost to His zealotry and mesmerism
and the country will soon follow

someday when they're less excited they'll admit
I knew better; I will not sit with folded hands

this work feels like the medicines I am given
thinking clear as glass, legs bouncing like horses

specific shove of the fervent mind
the certainty of my intolerances

when Nicky drops God's right hand
and stands there like a tree

I see the blue flame and lift
his hand burning back to the light

machinations of family are inadmissible
his mother said *It's Rasputin or me*

she lives in Denmark now
I haven't seen Ella since

The Outside World, their longing

a Greek chorus, a flock, a chatter of light
the girls have grown up, past books and nannies

they starve for the Outside World, its wonder
of soldier-boys who move so freely there

what are your cities like, your farms, how do
you go about? do you think of us here

as porcelain figurines inside an egg?
oh, they would fly from me if I opened my hands

so weary of being mothered and told
they would crack the sky with their becoming

Quieten me, promise, forgive, but it's for you I fight

managing Nicky through the war is the hardest
work I have done

write him long letters of advice every single day
so I stay a poultice on his mind

remind him his men are bullies
when I must bully him myself for every action

I send him things touched by Our Friend that he might absorb
the holy word from His comb, the apple that He held

he won't decide, he takes too long, he needs constant
pushing, he argues with the sense of my wishes

he ignores Our Friend's wisdom and asks me
not to report our conversations to Him

I must make him see that those who crush Our Friend
are like those who killed Christ

some of our advice he follows, but then
makes his own choices, tells me after by letter

oh the days of shrill writing it can take to change his mind
back, get him to sign his name

*

I have little choice but to follow my own course
and beg the master's forgiveness after

he makes me have the heart problems
and not sleep for my aching head

in a gesture of love and exhortation
I take the time from my work to travel to the front

I sit upon his desk
I hand him his pen

To hold what remains, a body lost and found

missing for some days, Our Friend is a figment
of vitriolic talk

there were such aggressive threats He cowered
a rabbit in a lightning storm

ranted His prophecy:
if He is killed our empire will soon collapse

now someone has seen His boots, one stuck in the bridge
railing, the other protruding from river ice

retrieved, He is bedraggled worse than life
stiff as an old cross, arms like Christ

three times murdered: poisoned, stabbed and drowned
we take Him into our lives as saviour a second time

buried nearby on our property
He is our secret once again

a shrine we can walk to from home
we bend over His rock and pray

They are out there, an ocean of drab fish

revolution has returned and masses outside our walls
surge of mindless need, farm weapons in hand

call me temptress and spy, bitch and whore
they want us dead at their feet

forgotten
their dedication by God to their Little Father on the throne

Nicky's Outside Children stamping for bread
and he like a fisher in a gilded iron boat

I pray it will get cold so the streets will clear
and the people remember what is needed

their warm woollen father
who also snaps the belt

the hooligans will be cleared like a snowfall
this country will be set to right

the work is hard, as stone is hard, and it crushes
what it must to please God; the work is hard

far from me, Nicky digs a way into his pillow every night
searching for feathers' deaf respite

As a dead holy man, his time on earth was short

without His breath, He is a political problem solved
a family embarrassment removed

those in this family who killed Him tell lies upon lies
blood in the yard a dog that needed killing

the police have stopped investigating
all Nicky can do is send them into exile

which of those murderers thought of Alexei
whose prayers will keep our boy alive now?

*

we are followed to His hidden grave
the ruined vessel of Him is unearthed

three more times they desecrate His holy form:
His severed manhood a trophy shown around town

His body burned away all night, His crumbling bones
left uncovered in the woods

even the earth does not know the spot
who but us will remember His name?

The scrim rises, a sketch of the world remains

where precisely is the tragedy
and its lessons, somewhere once beautiful?

a train crashing far behind us in the distance
is it ossified in the slumped body? is it

in the children, their curtained heads
of unasked questions?

is it ahead of us? come to wake us
with its stained-glass sutures

hope is the thing seen after you have put down
everything that makes you afraid

the story pieced together
blind adherents, blind adherence

neither of these could ever save the world
how late it is, when we learn anything

If he's coming home, it must be serious

I can't reach Nicky
my knees don't want to hold me up

letters don't go, rail and telegraph are taken over
newspapers not printing, banks shut

I feel like a bird at the top of an arc
that suspension before plummet

everything is silence or burst of shock
news of Nicky waylaid comes by men at the door

all classes of people throng with the workers
I pace window to window

thunder and shrill overtones in the streets, the sound
of war, but from rumbling bodies

*

upstairs my pack of kits blink in the feverish light
the girls deathly with measles, Alexei injured in bed

our detachment of guards are unsettled horses
with no master they creep toward the gate

Maria is the least sick, we go in our woollens
shake their hands, beg them to protect us

the affront of it, Nicky's troops refuse to shoot
Nicky's police refuse to shoot

Nicky's Cossacks hang red cloths from their bayonets
my orders go with his into this frail air

we are thin as ghosts
we are the news of the world

The children lie quiet in the dark, the lift does not work

I am done with my campaign of urging Nicky to act
a train has stopped

also stopped: a war, a marriage, a monarchy
a household

my husband has stopped like a watch
still as stone, flat of eye

like a prisoner of war, he is berated and kept awake
by dawn he has abdicated, on a gunpoint train

then he abdicates for Alexei, so he can't be taken
from us, and in case Nicky dies

I don't hear any of this for two days
I am hit by a flood of wind, a rain of blizzard

I am
lost in the vacant rooms of my head

*

a revolution does not stop
ideology of an afterlife, conducted by demons

electricity shut off
Alexei harboured upstairs in his wheeled chair

Misha is Tsar for one day
half of it he was sleeping and he didn't know

battered in his turn he also abdicates
because no-one can guarantee his life

*

this old heart does not stop
though, if there were ever a time

Like water off a duck's back, all is submission to God
Grand Duke Alexander Mikhailovich

Nicky tells those last days like diary entries
like the finished ends of his cigarettes

his mother and Misha's haranguing letters
like a chorus in robes, *abdicate, abdicate*

but it was ever going to be what God wanted
fatalist, the character drawn for him by the old playwright

*

acting like it was the last time, his mother visited Nicky
on that stalled train, held his bawling head in her lap

after his lightly pencilled
signature changed the world

*

I am now the age she was when her husband-King
died, ending her days as Empress of most of the world

after my wedding she kept the crown jewels
that the law of history meant her to pass to me

she bought me my own set, sent a box
a message I heard in the wrong ear

now I understand my true place
would I meekly walk behind Alexei's wife?

give a pinch-faced girl from a capricious country
my last vestige?

not on my screaming life
not even on Alexei's would I

And their King shall go into captivity

Amos 1:15

the Tsar makes a decision
Mr Romanov begins his journey home

train and war are resumed
he and I will have a lot of forgetting to do

my telegram is returned, blue-pencilled
there is no-one here by the name *Emperor*

*

the man who comes home is the one I ever loved
we eat with our five sick children

later he opens his jacket and shows me
his embalmed heart

*

to which body would I return, if I could?
my child-body doesn't remember me

yes, the one from our first year when I was a fish
a racehorse, a fox

nothing shy or indecisive
about Nicky's hands in my nightclothes

*

we are in our usual wing of Alexander Palace
house arrest (*for our safety*)

from the mobs and Bolsheviks
we are in the papers around the world

for being nobody
and still breathing

As the future ripens in the past,
so the past rots in the future—
a terrible festival of dead leaves

Anna Akhmatova

Alexander Palace, March

the Rule:
our commandant is a decent man
but the guards charge through the rooms
angry revolutionaries: they bait and goad
they hit Nicky with their gun butts, push him about
with their common dirty hands
blow smoke in my face and the girls'
staff who wish to remain are also under arrest
one of Alexei's bodyguards treats him like a bad dog
small vengeance for years the slave of a tyrant child
before he uses the newly opened door to join the revolution
Anna, caught in her sickroom burning papers
is dragged bodily to jail for collusion with Our Friend
at four p.m. they lock all the doors
the telephone lines are cut

the Light:
I finished with my crying yesterday

Alexander Palace, April

the Rule:
the servants must treat us as civilians
call us Mr and Mrs, call us *citizen*
we must speak only Russian
we may walk in the garden an hour or two
letters are censored both ways
Anastasia's window is shot at
when she hovers there thin as a curtain

the Light:
we are allowed out to the church on our grounds
we may have newspapers, our cameras
the wine stores and all three dogs
the girls' hair has fallen out from the measles
so they shave their heads and take laughing photographs
their sweet faces a row of moons

Alexander Palace, May

the Rule:
things are not so different from before
if we know anything as royals
we know cloister, its specific isolation
so easily mistaken for normalcy
I speak in fatalistic tones, God is testing us
I try to be a better woman, but my greatest sin
is my irritability, stupid people
stupid rules, requests denied
my untethered tongue a revolutionary

the Light:
prayers, then children's lessons in the mornings
the girls sit at windows watching for flashes of life
Nicky rereads the papers and chain-smokes
misses his hard walks and horse riding
here he settles for chopping ice and wood
otherwise his usual imperturbability

England will not save us, dearest George

cousin to both of us, declines our asylum
Granny would have flayed him

but the German problem of me in England
is too much for his legacy to bear

playmate since remembrance
friend and equal, on our side in the war

I am not surprised, I've heard a cruel man
grew up inside the body of that King

the King inside that man
full of his own hubris

historical Germans in every court of the world
are obliterating their dynasties

the house of Saxe-Coburg-Gotha now called Windsor
his father's name written out of time

God rest George's face, so much like Nicky's
they look like twins in all the photographs

would Nicky have done the same to him?
neither of them can ever know

Alexander Palace, June

the Rule:
a new commandant
as always some of the guards are black-souled heathens
now Nicky and I must keep to separate rooms
all day and night, except meals
lest we conspire under their ignorant noses
with our five languages
sleeping apart exquisitely enrages me
I speak German to see them squirm
they take Alexei's toy rifle
he cries like a child much younger than twelve

the Light:
the staff still love us
some of the guards are good boys
we plant a kitchen garden

Nothing can come but what God wills

Thomas More

who runs our suffering country week to week
changes like a comedy

Lenin comes, Lenin goes
once there was no government at all

our commandants change apace
every boy in Russia has been our guard

I can think of no historical state of calm
to which Russia could return

was it not wild dark men hitting with sticks
before autocracy and Romanovs?

what Russia ever was, a raging petulance
of poverty and hideous royalty

when we arrived the sky had already
been shot full of holes

All our things, an island of war trophies

I wonder what Monsieur Fabergé will do, now that
he won't make me my Easter-time eggs anymore

those tiny fantastics of engineering and magic, those
encrusted, ostentatious gifts from Nicky

they took all year to design and make, each one
more astonishing than the last

all are tossed with the art off our walls
our silver and linens and china

in some dark Bolshevik storeroom
a toppled Easter hunt for mad rebels

those delicacies of pure thought, gold hinges opening
on wee marvels, those bejewelled manifestations of us

I'd have eaten them from egg cups with a spoon
if I'd known such disdain would befall them

poor family of beauties, poor lost work of an artist
arrayed on the mantel in memory's firing line

Alexander Palace, July

the Rule:
five months locked in here
the Bolsheviks gain strength
they are preferred by the people to any version
of the old brocaded world order
now we must be moved (*for our safety*)
we ask for our summer palace far to the south
but are told to pack warm clothes
we must justify the need for each staff person
at ten p.m. the electricity is turned off
the doors to our rooms upstairs locked
we wait in our coats, seated on our trunks
in the vestibule all night
Nicky's estranged brother comes
they stand stiffly as men, without talking
I wonder, from my weeping-corner, if Nicky regrets
exiling Misha for marrying a commoner
so small our previous disappointments

the Light:
if it can be called light, we burn our private papers
our thoughts overthrown, unavailable to history

Where the sun stays awake, the White Nights of summer

since the beginning it has happened this way
sky a misted river all night, dim ball of sun

detained on the horizon
God-like glow from the top of the world

its hem sweeping the ground
trees look like etchings of themselves

Russians out late, children reading all hours
curtains accordingly thick

all earth's birds wing-still
inherently knowing night from day

the pages of the book clear
the message unreadable

Tobolsk, August

the Rule:
days in a mountain-struggling train, then a steamer
we are going to Tobolsk in Siberia
no roads or rail, only the summer river in or out
we sail past the house of Our Friend
God is brightly near us
I feel Our departed Friend calls us here for a reason
seven more days living in the yacht
house is found boarded up, filthy, without furniture
the guards here are boys from the factories
Bolshevik in pay only

the Light:
Freedom House they call it, on Freedom Road
we laugh out loud despite dire exhaustion
irony may be the only sweetness left

Tobolsk, September

the Rule:
the staff must live in another house
newspapers and letters sporadic and out of date
if taken to church in town, all the way is lined
shoulder to shoulder, a corridor of guards
the toilets break and overflow
the property is fenced tight and high all around
when not allowed to church the priest
comes to the front hall

the Light:
Nicky and I may sleep together again
we still look through our photographs
they hurt in suffocating ways
here, those two Alexei took
so graceful they could have been sold as postcards
and this one of Anastasia before her mirror
taking a snapshot of herself, taking a snapshot of herself

The books left open, as if the reader will shortly return

the papers say one of our homes
has been made into a museum

people pay to walk through
and look at the objects that were

lately our extant lives
there should be a rule

that to be an artifact
one must be dead

at least deaf and blind
at least missing

there is no refuge
even from our latent selves

Tobolsk, October

the Rule:
the Bolsheviks take power
another new commandant
no more going to church
the priest comes when allowed
all Romanovs are under house arrest
except Nicky's mother and sisters who escaped Russia
now we must carry identity cards about the prison house
show on demand
we may not close any doors
guards jeer into bedrooms and bathrooms

the Light:
if I had my paints here
I would paint the garden at this house
its violet-pigmented hour
my mind's curtained church
I would not paint the hard-faced guards
who tramp within its confines
what came before this, I can't remember

Tobolsk, November–December

the Rule:
winter is below zero in our rooms
this house has no heating system but fireplaces
frozen wind blows in the window frames
with cramped hands I knit our socks
under-linens worn to rags, the girls dress like maids

the priest is arrested
for calling us Majesty, his mistake
a tiny gift of candlelight to warm us

the Light:
we make a Christmas as best we can, decorate a tree
make gifts and sweets for our good guards
the smell of fir and woodsmoke through the house
is the ancient air from which we are formed
at night we listen into the beyond
for our oracles to send comfort
sleep a brief window of forgetting

if these boys don't all die before this is over, may God
make them good fathers one day
we seven make a ring of indelible love
all things for us are in the past
the future a disruption in the fog

Life here is nothing, eternity is everything

a cage of moonglow wakes me every hour
burning hot in my blankets

dreams I can't remember, nightmare state
of dread, impotence sluicing my veins

with boiling water—I lie awake preparing
my soul for the kingdom of heaven

I would get up and read, but my reading glasses
are downstairs and the lights are not allowed on

Nicky breathes on beside me, his dreams sequestered
the tobacco smell of his beard keeps me alive

clocktick, moonslide, something clicks like a gun barrel inside
the body and then I feel cold—a deserted city, a horizon

I retrieve the blankets and begin again, hold his drifted body
like a raft, an unseen day breaking somewhere near

Tobolsk, January, 1918

the Rule:
order sustains us:
prayers, then lessons, walk one hour
occupy ourselves in our rooms
tea at four, puzzles, games
dinner at eight, Nicky reads aloud to us, bed

the Light:
with the guards Nicky and the children
build an ice mountain for sledding
they come in bruised and happy
smelling of winter

Tobolsk, February

February the Bolsheviks have stopped time
Russia follows the Gregorian calendar now
I don't care what the rest of the world does
we've just lost two weeks of our biographies
fourteen days unwritten, unlived
a thready uncertainty hums behind all that we do
the guards are ordered to destroy the ice mountain
atop, we can see over the fence

the Light:
when we return to it, the world will be

Alexei, that angry boy of boys

just when he is well, the boy in him jumps
or climbs and is injured again

now he has sledded indoors, this child!
roaring and bashing himself

down the staircase like a bolt of cloth
his body is his own to hurt

that ineffable need of bleeders to be reckless
to pursue the free boy locked inside

his lesson of rage and boredom and mercy
teaches the guards nothing

a swampy ball of blood balloons the groin
atrophies the leg nerves

even if the blood should stop pumping
the leg may never walk again

what can I do about such angry innocence
that taste for iron in the mouth?

Tobolsk, March

the Rule:
they take Alexei's wooden dagger
our personal capital is reduced
more staff are sent away
we are put on soldiers' rations
a machine gun is set up across the street
points its black eye at our balcony

the Light:
Alexei makes a bow and arrow
townspeople send butter, coffee and jam

The new Russia is all words and noise

I feel sorry for those idealists who are good people
this country's starved and mutinous

wading into their grey tragedy
I will thank God when their eyes are opened

Nicky can't believe the Bolsheviks took us out of the war
gave away the Crimea, our summer palace there

Germany negotiates for our living persons, a joke
if anything were funny anymore

we would rather die in Russia than be saved
by the Germans after all they've done to us

they would save us for their own purposes
better a constitutional monarchy than Bolshevism

there is a civil war, white counter-revolutionaries
red Bolsheviks with their flags rearing up everywhere

Tobolsk, April, week 1

the Rule:
a new commandant
we are astonished and horrified—another move
(*for our safety*) but we cannot with Alexei
bleeding still, again, as ever
Nicky will be removed immediately
to prevent rescue
or to stand trial in Moscow
which in any language translates to execution
the fit I take is for the ages
I must choose my bedridden child
or accompany my husband to his possible death
I am excoriated. I twist from focus.
they will less likely kill him if he is not alone

the Light:
Marie and I will go with him
the other girls will nurse Alexei
when the river thaws and opens
they will join us by steamer
we sit at Alexei's bedside all night
as if at our own funeral

Tobolsk, April, week 2

the Rule:
the commandant escorts us personally
overland, because the frozen river
is a Godless impasse to nowhere
we may take little luggage, meagre provisions
it is April, but nothing like spring
we may send letters to the children
we are code named *The Baggage*

the Light:
is impossible to discern from here

Tomorrow, what blessed awful thing will befall

we leave our children behind; God help
us and our captors' promises of their lives

we travel like animals to market in a peasant cart
a bed of straw, false mercy of an old mattress

our meaty bodies smashed to soup bones
over rutted frozen ground or wheel-breaking mud

if there is anything beautiful left in this country
it is in the mind's eye of another woman's life

horses to their chests in icy streams, then one miraculous
filthy stinking train, flat of floor and not a farm buggy

how many days a perforated, rattled mind
sorting anguish from discomfort

how many hours wishing for nothing more than stillness
my hands hard and red from hanging on

by the station signs we see: not Moscow after all
but deeper into Siberia: Ekaterinburg

*

the word *Bolshevik* like a gob of sick from the lungs
taste of rot in the mouth

this prison is smaller, matryoshka houses going down
fence of tight staves reaches to the second floor

days awash in my new sickbed, the head
a splitting ball of stars and too much noise

sky a blurred dome, unable to promise redemption
how often lately I think of rapture

my soul a new peaceful sound
lifting upward from the narrow bell of my skirt

Ekaterinburg, May, week 1

the Rule:
the commandant at Ipatiev House is a decent man
his deputy is the devil's worst son
he searches our luggage for days touching
every bookmark and pill and shoe
we sit with nothing till it pleases him
the floor plan Nicky drew to send the children
is confiscated
it could be used to hatch a rescue plot
from this House of Special Purpose
walks are brief and arbitrary
an old man comes and whitewashes the windows
then nails them shut

the Light:
we can just see the tops of the church cupolas
we can hear the bells

Something, not love, returned them to us

in the steamship that brings the children to us
a story of vodka and hammers and nails

the men and Alexei are nailed like cargo
behind their cabin doors for the night

they will hear for the rest of their lives
the women screaming, our girls amongst

yelling, hooting insults of unsupervised men
acting out a historical anger

we can't bring ourselves to deface
our girls with the telling

soldiers so drunk they could capsize the boat
their lurching and thrusting

with the many engines of night
they punish the girls in our place

terrorize them, sitting up in their dresses
all night for scant safety

doors of their cabins removed from their hinges
what may or may not have happened there

*

Olga sits still at the blanked-out window
a bruise-eyed wraith

somewhere out there is a soldier she loved
we don't discuss the state of her heart

Ekaterinburg, May, week 2

the Rule:
the children are not given their beds for days
Alexei hurts himself deliberately and wails
for nights in his familiar landscape of pain
his two men-in-waiting and his doctor
denied residence with us
the doctor may visit once a day
with a visitor's pass, a guard at his elbow

the Light:
we are all together whatever God may ask of us next
the garden is a bursting of blossom and leaf
the air not at all like civil war

Now, we are no longer allowed cream

even in this most egg-like of Inside Lives, we have secrets
a letter, folded small in the top of the cream bottle

'monarchists' planning a daring rescue ask a thousand
enthusiastic questions: where do we sleep? is there a window?

they will smuggle in morphine to knock the boy out
they will storm the house and point guns

we must be ready to climb down a rope of bedsheets
from a second-floor window at the urgent moment

the tone of the guards' watching has changed
they whisper when we reach for writing paper

we sit blinking at the absurdity and decline
our devoted staff would be left behind

five weakened women, an unconscious weight
of boy to be lowered in a heavy sling

but just in case, we sit up nights dressed and ready
torturous *nothing* happens

telephones have been ringing in the guardhouse
for days, the boy guards are sent away

we realize we've capitulated to hope
and its small borrowed truths

Ekaterinburg, June, week 1

the Rule:
arrested Romanovs are transferred from
all over Russia to a hotel here in Ekaterinburg
something unspeakable may be about to happen
like an owl dropping, folded, from the sky
Nicky's brother Misha was taken from prison
but did not arrive here
the sky is walking in its white sleep
these rooms are a vow of silence
what happened to Misha?

the Light:
I find I have forgiven Ella, so near me now
if only in flesh and not spirit
and Anna with her gifts and letters, coded hints
of real rescue endeavours in the making
the White Army is arriving, we would collapse
into their hands as into a bed of clouds

Ekaterinburg, June, week 2

the Rule:
we eleven must ludicrously stand
for roll call every morning
Alexei needs him daily, but now the doctor
may or may not come
paling stockade is urgently built higher
machine-gun sound of pounding nails
the kitchen further heats the hot summer house
we ask for windows open, refused
we ask for one window open, refused

the Light:
a moment of false hope when walks through:
the *Committee for the Examination of the Question*
of Windows in the House of Special Purpose

List, my shifting trinities

three: brother, sister, mother all dead of my amnesia
three: Papa, brother, and Father Above wrapping me like raiment

three: God and Granny and Nicky pulling me like a knot
three I did not imagine: husband, son, Our departed Friend

now, all dark uncertainties await, same deaf sky overhead
three: houses of imprisonment

head full of prayer cards, crisply shuffling
my son no longer looks like he will live forever

Ekaterinburg, June, week 3

the Rule:
the guards here are no older than our girls

the Light:
what they find is not
Nicholas the Bloody, not the *German Bitch*
but a greying couple
pinched in place
four breathlessly lovely girls
angling for any happiness
we ask them to play cards
they sit with the girls and dogs
look through our photograph albums
they look like so many actors
performing laughter and flirting
like a play of some family's life

We live as on a ship at sea, the days all alike

Nicholas Romanov

I was in love at nineteen, I should remember it
when thinking of Maria's birthday

another incident we do not write down
but leave to others' pens

the soldier-boy's name is Ivan
he fairly drops his gun when she passes

she feels a future moving inside her body
like the moon

or a small animal waking up to itself
he smuggles in for her a birthday cake

in the happy chatter the two vanish, a stir of stomping
guards finds them behind a door, ashen faced

their bodies are slow with terror, but their eyes
are epiphanies

*

Ivan is taken ill and never returns
Maria has put us all in danger

she weeps and wonders if he is dead
lies awake imagining their unborn children

the rescue he will single-handedly perform
lowering her from the window by her long hair

Olga and I punish her with silence and averted eyes
her rash and immoral act under God's eye

fraternizing guards and commandant disappear
the new leader so feral, his eyes freeze us in place

Ekaterinburg, June, week 4

the Rule:
walks may or may not be curtailed
guards bark along at our heels
the priest does not come
our cameras are locked up
with our confiscated trunks in the barn
we are allowed only enough meat now for soup

the Light:
the Whites want us removed alive
the Reds want something more Biblical
we hear artillery moving in the streets
our captors are agitated

Ekaterinburg, July, week 1

the Rule:
this new commandant
black of eye and hair
black of soul
is a fixer of messes
from the soldiers he returns our pilfered
possessions, locks into a box our cash money
the plain rings and bracelets off our bodies
what does the whispering mean
code name *Chimney Sweep*?
Alexei's last bodyguard is taken away
the new guards are slabs of wood
they do not look us in the eyes

the Light:
one window is opened, whitewash removed
a heavy iron grille is placed over
sky still imaginary, but delicious air

When dawn opens like a sash, a moment of blank

I recall all that has happened in painful cascade
long lists of unjust acts, and we

still imprisoned
tedious fabric of our humiliated lives

my blood runs cold as if I've been sitting in dirt
entire days have gone abject, how much worse?

our remaining riches smuggled this far
enough jewels left to buy a quiet exile

our ten soft hands sewing for months
collateral stitched between the bones of our corsets

into belts and hatbands, seams and false buttons
ready to move, empty handed, at a moment's notice

familiar handwork for confiscated days
bright bands of soreness to adorn our ribs

Blight of moon, corset of pine staves around

we abide in this terrible locked egg of stark workings
spring has moved into summer, the closed house

a suffocating teapot, God gone quiet overhead
we love differently here

only hands, only on each other's hearts
the machine of our breathing passing back and forth

this one only life, ever punctuated by blood
and bleeding, our catastrophic history

this house a void through which some hopeful rescue
may yet still pass

a dim external life where we imagine
ourselves on earth, in our thin beautiful skins

God reappearing from memory's ruin
stepping into plain fresh air

and walking somewhere
our names gone simple on the tongue

We live here on earth, already half gone to the next world

after three months here Nicky stops writing his diary
his lifelong eleven p.m., bare facts of his day

he is a toy run out of its winding key
the veil of his eyes frightens me

after months of only vespers
the priest performs a full mass

it could be a delivery of hope
it could be last rites

the room smells of gratitude
and hunting clothes

Nicky's last entry: *481 days, the weather is warm and pleasant*
we have absolutely no news from the outside

Ekaterinburg, July, week 3

the Rule:
the atmosphere around us is fairly electrified

the Light:
though the storm is coming nearer and nearer
our souls are at peace

A dream, all bloody rags and elbows

… as if I am an owl watching from a high branch
it is deep forest and far north of home

summer sky a twilit hand whitening the night
we are disarticulated puppets thrown down

a dirty hole, our dry mouths caught open in the telling
eggshell eyes

faces smashed, garments and bodies burned
we are a making

of ruins—fall in, fall in
the bullets a blessing in retrospect

our spirits free to mill amongst the tree trunks
our voices, opalescent, underground …

Acknowledgements

My thanks go to the historians and biographers and aggregators who came before me and provided the dozens of books and websites I read over the decades preceding the writing of these poems. As the 100th anniversary of the Russian Revolution and the murder of the Romanovs approached, there was a swath of new publications I added to my research.

I am grateful to the Manitoba Arts Council for financial support. Thanks to the team at the Porcupine's Quill: Stephanie Small for the discussions and assiduous editing of the poems; Chandra Wohleber for the excellent copy-editing and proof-reading; and Tim and Elke Inkster for the gorgeous layout and art.

My interest in the Romanovs began with a mother's firsthand knowledge of hemophilia in my own family tree. It has been discovered that the bleeding disorder that Queen Victoria spread through Europe is hemophilia B. Though my family originates from neighbouring Slavic regions it is hemophilia A that runs in my blood.

I have used two Anna Akhmatova quotes: the one on page 9 is from a translation by A. S. Kline; the other on page 81 is from a translation by Stanley Kunitz with Max Hayward.

'Blight of moon, corset of pine staves around' appeared in *Prairie Fire: Everyday Love* vol. 39, no. 1. A version of 'When the sun wakes up, a bluish-white heavenly body' appears in the anthology *Heartwood: Poems for the Love of Trees*, 2018, published by the League of Canadian Poets.

Lori Cayer is the author of three previous poetry collections, *Dopamine Blunder* (Tightrope, 2016), *Attenuations of Force* (Frontenac House, 2010) and *Stealing Mercury* (The Muses' Company, 2004). A winner of the John Hirsch Award for Most Promising Manitoba Writer and of the Eileen McTavish Sykes Award for Best First Book, she is a former co-editor of *Contemporary Verse 2* and is co-founder of the Lansdowne Prize for Poetry. Her poetry is endlessly informed by her editorial work in scientific research publishing. She lives in Winnipeg.